Cuisines *From* India & Abroad

Delectable, Relishing and Ravishing

Asha Rani Vohra

V&S PUBLISHERS

Published by:

V&S PUBLISHERS

F-2/16, Ansari road, Daryaganj, New Delhi-110002
☎ 23240026, 23240027 • *Fax:* 011-23240028
Email: info@vspublishers.com • *Website:* www.vspublishers.com

Regional Office : Hyderabad
5-1-707/1, Brij Bhawan (Beside Central Bank of India Lane)
Bank Street, Koti, Hyderabad - 500 095
☎ 040-24737290
E-mail: vspublishershyd@gmail.com

Branch Office : Mumbai
Jaywant Industrial Estate, 1st Floor–108, Tardeo Road
Opposite Sobo Central Mall, Mumbai – 400 034
☎ 022-23510736
E-mail: vspublishersmum@gmail.com

Follow us on: 🇹 🇫 in

DISCLAIMER

CONTENTS

Publisher's Note

The Indian housewife today is no longer the same as she was in the bygone days, who spent half of her life working in the kitchen with a back bent. Except for cooking, women of olden age living in the interior of their houses had no direct connection with their guests and almost no ambition in life.

Now she is a conscious housewife or a working woman, useful for the society. Progress in science and technology has made her world trouble-free. She herself wants to move with the times. She wishes to do her work better with the help of scientific equipments, technological ways and means, and gives her work an artistic touch, thus saving her labour and time which can be utilised further for other useful purposes. Such a training includes essential knowledge about food, efficient running of the kitchen and looking after it properly, cleanliness while cooking and serving food artistically, welcoming of guests and all modern etiquettes pertaining to it.

There are other books on culinary art and recipes available in the market. But this book is different from them.

How is it different and unique?

This book does not have a spate of recipes of vegetables, pickles, *chutneys*, *murabbas*, sweets, etc., as found in other books. An attempt has been made to cater to the metropolitan as well as the small town housewives. They face day to day problems about what to serve. To promote national integration and to bring about international closeness, the emphasis nowadays is on a menu of different kinds of cuisine. This book presents this untrodden field in a beautiful way. The various delicious dishes are substantiated with lots of relevant pictures and an exclusive **tip off** at the bottom of each recipe.

The *Cuisines From India & Abroad* contains *mouth-watering recipes* with their ingredients and methods of preparation, special tip-offs and all the exclusive characteristics as mentioned above.

A Language of ThePlates

"She cooks beautifully …she is so clean and efficient in her cooking…she serves in such a pleasing manner that one feels like praising her to the skies. There seems to be some magic in her hands."

You must have been showered with such praises now and then and felt elated about them.

Taste of food and its attractive presentation– in other words pleasure of the palate and feast for the eyes- are at par, as far as eating goes. Food may be very palatable, nutritious, but if its presentation is not such that it can speak out to the eater, then all the money and labour spent on it becomes meaningless. Satisfaction from eating should be accompanied by a language.

You may be very good at cooking. The quality of cooking, eye on neatness and cleanliness while cooking, correct method of cooking to preserve the food values, coupled with the tastes of the eaters, breaking of monotony in the menu, and above all, an attractive way of serving – all these combine to speak of your culinary art.

This book is different from other cookery books, being devoted to the art of presenting food in a way which pleases the eyes, along with the recipes of some new and special dishes. Emphasis is on the recipes of a few selected dishes, along with suggestions about serving them attractively – every item has been substantiated by a picture.

Due to the developments in the field of science and technology, there are innumerable special dishes in an Indian menu. It is not possible to include all these recipes in a small pictorial book. But some nutritious and delicious dishes have been incorporated, particularly from different parts of the country. Methods for serving them attractively are also given along with the ingredients and the cooking style.

These are mere suggestions, because the same dish can be cooked and served in various artistic ways. With this belief in mind, the book is dedicated and presented to you. Hope it serves its purpose to enlighten the cook in you. Try out the new and interesting recipes given in the book. *Enjoy cooking and enjoy eating*!

PART - 1

ART OF COOKING

*I*n a modern society, stress is laid on how the food tastes as well as how it is presented. So every young lady these days is keen to learn this art through cookery classes in domestic science courses, books, magazines and periodicals.

In Indian homes, sitting on a wooden stool or plank or floor, eating in metal plates and sitting on a chair and eating on a dining table, are prevalent side by side. But eating in the kitchen is confined within the family and eating at a table sitting on a chair is preferred when the guests have to be entertained. Now in urban life, eating on dining table is becoming more popular day by day in almost every home and the old custom of feeding the guests seated on the floor is almost extinct.

Ancient Indian Custom

Due to lack of space, if feeding a large number of guests on the floor is convenient to you, first of all, clean the floor thoroughly. Then spread druggets or mats in long rows and place wooden stools in front. If guests are too many in number and you are short of stools, use wooden planks instead. Cover them with clean white sheets. If that also is not possible, you may place the plates on the floor with *Alpana* or *Rangoli* designs. Flowers also may be used to decorate the place. If the food is to be served on leaf plates or plantain leaves, they should be cleaned thoroughly.

If the food is served on plates, put as much of it as can be consumed, so that there is no wastage in these days of soaring prices. You may serve more than once, but do not force food on your guests or serve them even after they say no. Your art of serving will be judged by how efficiently you serve the food on a plate, how you serve the further helping, how warm your behaviour is while welcoming guests and also how you have decorated the place.

So this art of hosting and serving has also to be taken care of, besides cooking attractive and palatable dishes.

Modern Method

These days most of the households do not have so many stools or planks and the above kind of entertaining is not in vogue. The Western style of eating on table and chair has become a part and parcel of our lives now. Taking note of the changing times and also convenience, there is no harm in adopting it. These days training in the art of serving is based on this method. So it is necessary to learn and imbibe it in your day to day cooking.

Tip off

In ancient Indian custom, the food used to be served on the floor in the kitchen. This was like an open kitchen of the modern times.

A modern kitchen has facilities for cooking while standing. This avoids getting up every time a thing is needed. No bending either. This way food can be cooked faster and more conveniently. It is less tiring, rather energy conserving, dress does not get muffled up and no fear of fire with children around. So, a kitchen should be planned with shelves all around and a table or a platform should be there for cooking in standing position. Have closed cabinets instead of open shelves for storage and a cupboard with iron mesh to keep milk, curd, vegetables etc., in case you do not have a refrigerator. This will add to cleanliness and comfort in the kitchen. Slabs made of concrete, chips or cement should be against two walls and two and a half feet above the ground.

Place the stove, or gas burner or cooking range on one side and all other necessary things in the closed cabinets below the platform or on the wall. Since everything will be handy this way, work will be easier and less time consuming. Place a deep sink for washing utensils on the other side of the wall, or in the centre, or in a corner. The tap should be on top and proper arrangements should be made for the flow of water. Make a mesh cabinet with a rack to keep washed plates on the upper part. Rest of the utensils can be kept on a slanting, narrow plank near the sink, for the water to drain out easily.

There should be some vacant space nearby, to be used for chopping vegetables, kneading flour and such jobs. Things to be used for these may be kept in a cabinet and cleaned properly for a healthy and hygienic cooking. There should also be adequate ventilation in the kitchen, so an exhaust fan or a chimney is a must.

Tip off

A kitchen equipped with all amenities is like a modern car of today equipped with all the latest gadgets. Isn't it?

*Y*our family's health depends on the cleanliness of your kitchen and your convenience while cooking depends on how well equipped your kitchen is. Hence, equal attention should be paid to both these aspects.

Arrangement for proper light and air in the kitchen is essential along with the rest of the décor. There should be a window in front of the door for cross ventilation and the platform for cooking should be a little away from it. Water outlet if not adequate can result in the floor well becoming full of dirt and a breeding ground for germs. Walls and roof should be whitewashed once or twice a year. Walls should not be infested with cobwebs.

Clean the shelves and the floor after every meal. Add insecticides once or twice a week in the water used for sweeping the floor.

Scrub the place used for washing utensils with any detergent and a brush. In case there is no proper drainage of water from washed utensils, fix a sheet of aluminium or rubber there and add a small spoon of ammonia in the water used for cleaning the kitchen platform. This will remove greasiness. Doors and windows of the kitchen should have iron mesh, to prevent flies from entering. The garbage tin should have a lid. Burn waste paper once a week in the empty metal bin to avoid the danger of catching germs.

Change the dusters of the kitchen frequently and wash them with antiseptic soap or any detergent. Keep all the food items always covered. With such care, there will be no fear of contracting diseases. Cleanliness of the kitchen is absolutely essential for you and your family's health.

Tip off

Sunlight and fresh air kill germs. Arrange for proper ventilation in your kitchen, by providing it with an exhaust or chimney.

All women cook at homes and even men are good cooks, these days. So it is not necessary to tell them the basics. The most important question is whether the food prepared has a thought behind it, or is it done casually? Are the nutritional values kept intact scientifically, or emphasis is only on taste? Are factors like saving of time, labour and money taken into account while cooking or half of one's life is spent fretting and fuming while working in the kitchen. It is important to give a thought to all these. For efficient cooking, the following tips may be kept in mind.

Keep all necessary things handy and keep them at their proper places after use, so that you do not waste time looking for them again and again.

Use double burner gas stove, or a cooking range for your convenience and faster cooking.

Mechanical Gadgets

To save labour, invest money in mechanical gadgets once. Such an investment pays in the long run. Save money out of your entertainment budget, or spend a little less on clothes and equip yourself with some gadgets like gas, heater, cooker, toaster, immersion rod for hot water, mixie, oven, etc. Besides these, having a fridge in the kitchen is convenient. Things like

geyser can wait. If none of these can be obtained, get at least a stove, cooker and an icebox for yourself. Similarly, if the kitchen is not conveniently built or renovation is not possible, get a big table made. Below the table, closed cabinet on one side and mesh cabinet on the other side may be made for storage. A stone slab or metal sheet can be placed on the top, where the gas or stove is kept. You will gain by saving time and buy the convenience.

Keep a special eye on cleanliness and tidiness while cooking. Everything should be covered. Your hands and dusters should be clean. Do not spill water and scatter garbage all around. Their places should be properly specified.

Arrange all the necessary things before lighting the burner for cooking so that there is no wastage of fuel, oil, gas and electricity.

Cook Well

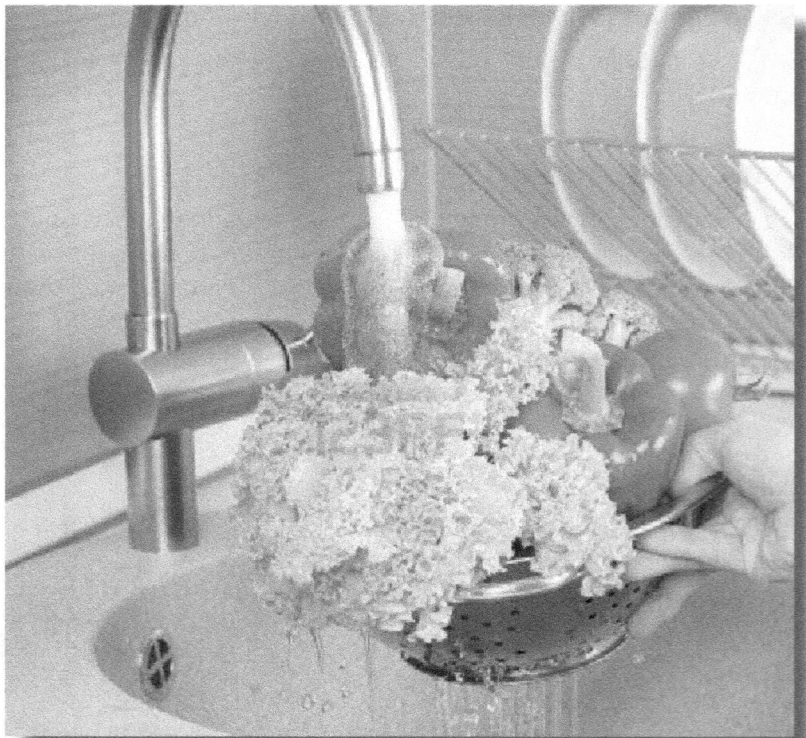

Wash the vegetables before chopping. They lose their mineral salts if washed afterwards. Green leafy vegetables should be definitely washed before chopping. While cooking, care should be taken that the nutritive value and natural taste is not lost in the process. Cook vegetables in steam. If it is necessary to drain water after boiling, use this water in *dal* or cooking pulses. Do not throw away the starchy rice water after draining. Use enough water to cook rice, which gets absorbed during cooking. This way vegetables and rice will not lose their nutritive value. If cottage cheese (paneer) is made at home, use its water in *dal* and vegetables. Clean the wheat well before grinding. Do not sift the wheat flour. You will lose vitamins E and B with the remnants. Whole pulses (*dals*) should be used as far as possible.

Cooking on a high flame harms food values resulting in the loss of vitamins. Most of the food can be cooked on low or medium fire. Food values remain intact if the food is cooked in cookers.

Cook soft vegetables with skin. Cook them in steam or boil them. Some vegetables can be eaten raw. If you prefer vegetables fried in ghee, do not use too much spices. Fry them enough, so that their juices do not burn out.

One should be energetic and attentive while cooking. Cleanliness, saving time and labour, efficiency, all have their importance. You may utilize the extra time saved for some other purpose. Wash your hands well and use a little moisturizer or hand cream after your cooking is over. Take care of your hands and get the nails manicured once a week or fortnightly, so that the stains of vegetables and dirt after washing do not show in the cracks of your hands. It is absolutely essential to keep the nails clean.

So, keeping the nutritive values of food intact while cooking, saving of time, labour and fuel, cleanliness and neatness – all these combined together make for a scientific and technical way of cooking.

Tip off

Few extra things helpful in cleanliness and safety:

➤ Burnol
➤ Hand lotion
➤ Hand cream
➤ Soap, Vim
➤ Brush for cleaning bottles
➤ A piece of sponge to clean the sink and buckets
➤ Mop to sweep the floor
➤ Two hand towels — one near the sink and the other in the kitchen for wiping hands
➤ Napkin
➤ A low wooden plank, for standing on it while using an electric heater

*D*elicious food may not seem palatable if it is not served properly. So the art of serving and table decoration is as important as the culinary art itself.

If you have a separate dining room, it should be well ventilated and lighted. Paint the walls with colours pleasing to the eyes. Put bright curtains, but the colour should not be too dark. The lampshades should have pretty colours and the bulbs should not be very bright during dinner. These days candle light dinners are highly appreciated. A beautiful candle stand can be used for this purpose, or a dimly lit chandelier can be hung from the ceiling.

If there is no separate dining room, the *verandah* adjacent to the kitchen can be enclosed, decorated and converted into a small dining room. Otherwise place the dining table and chairs on one side of your living room. If the living room is longish, a different colour or a standing screen partition can be put in the middle, to give this portion the look of a separate room.

If your living room is small and separate dining area cannot be carved out of it, use a small folding table. Put it on one side of the room and expand it, when necessary, to be used as a dining table A few chairs and puffies, etc. can be put around it . The multi-purpose folding table can be used as a centre table also. Four to six people can use it together at a time conveniently.

Decoration of the Dining Table

While writing about the decoration of the dining table, we assume that you have table with atleast four to six chairs around it. If arrangements have to be made for large number of guests, many such tables can be put in an open space. They can be hired. It is evident that such an arrangement is necessary only for big formal parties or functions. A few guests frequenting your home can be entertained on your dining table.

Cover this table with clean, washed, ironed white sheet. Then arrange artistically embroidered or painted table mats on it. One set of mats has 13 pieces – 1 big long mat to place the serving bowls in the centre, six middle sized mats for plates and six small mats for side plates. Arrange them in such a way that in front of every chair, the middle sized mat is on the right and the small is on the left of them. They should be placed side by side.

Now place big and small plates on them in the same order. Put glasses on the right side, on the upper side of the big plate. Put two spoons on the right side of each plate. If soup is to be served, a big soup spoon should also be provided. Tablespoons should be used for eating rice. If knives and forks are to be used for eating, these also should be placed in an organized way. So put small and big spoons, fork and knife together, near each plate and put a napkin too. Decorate the centre or around the serving bowls with flower arrangements on the table. Whether you use a bouquet of flowers or decorate the table in the Ikebana style or

with Rangoli, depends on your own good taste and sense. Salt and pepper cellars, bottles of sauce, *chutney* and pickles should be arranged neatly between the serving bowls.

Decorating Napkins on the Table

Make napkins out of thick cotton material. White, light pink or lemon coloured materials can be used. They should be absolutely clean, washed, starched and ironed. Fold them into eight squares or triangles and place them on the big plates, or shape them into flowers and place them in the empty glasses. They may be folded like caps or boats and kept on the table. This art is an important part of table decoration and must be learnt.

A Few More Designs For You to Learn

1.   Napkin flowers in the glasses placed on a long table, can be made thus:

    Hold the lower edge of the napkin with four folds. Fold the edge a bit and stick it in the glass. Now out of the four folds lower the two on the side and shape like two open leaves by bringing the four folds lower the two on the side and shape like two open leaves by bringing the pointed edges in front. Now open the centre leaves opposite to each other. It will look like a *blossoming flower*. It is easy to do it, if the napkin is well starched.

2. There are more methods of decorating napkins.

   To make this design, double up ⌐-fold napkin from the centre. Make a triangle and turn the lower portion upside down as shown in the photograph. Now keep it on the plate or near it. Place it upside down. It looks beautiful.

3. To make a design that looks like the cap of a waiter:

   Fold the napkin into eight and turn two folds in one direction and two in the opposite direction fixing the two edges to each other. When opened, it will be a boat like cap. Place it on the plate or near it.

4. The design in the centre is made with two napkins:

   Spread a doubly folded napkin. Then gather the whole napkin, like saree folds. Double it from the lower edge and fix in the glass. It will look like an open fan. This single design can be used. To make the other design shown here, fold another napkin starting from one corner. Fold it double and fix in the glass. The back side should be seen from the rear part of the first napkin and the front should be below the fan. Turn the face in front and open it a bit. There will be a dancing peacock in the glass. Napkins can be decorated in many ways. You may experiment with new designs. Guests open up these napkins to spread on their knees, after they sit down to eat. Before that, these napkins add to the beauty of the table.

Sweet dishes can be decorated in many ways with chopped almonds, pistachio, cherries, silver wrapping, cardamom powder, saffron, etc. You can decorate a plate according to the festival, function and occasion. Here you have to show your entire artistic talent.

Sweets can also be decorated in a special way on Diwali for the entire family. Mango leaves and a coconut can be placed on the auspicious pot. Fruits are decorated on a plantain Rangoli design around them and lighted lamps on mats with Batik designs add to the beauty.

If you invite a newly married couple for a meal, a different kind of decoration on the dining table can present a light humour, along with an important piece of advice. The whole atmosphere is bound to become cheerful. You can make four figures made out of boiled potatoes of a man woman, a boy and a girl and decorate them with cloves (eyes), cardamom powder (clothes, etc.) tomato rings (caps) and cabbage leaves (veil). Black pepper powder can be used instead of cardamom for this salad.

Similarly cartoons, dolls, birds, animals, Santa Claus, boy doll and girl doll, etc. can be made out of potatoes, thickened milk and other ingredients for a children's party. The party will be more enjoyable for children and the guests will be delighted. You will be showered with praises.

But decoration of food preparations should not be given importance only on special occasions or parties. You should incorporate this art in your daily life too to make your food more attractive and alluring. Decorate dishes of vegetables, salads, rice plate, custard, pudding, etc. Salad decorations should be experimented with, every day. A separate chapter has been devoted to it in the coming pages. Decorate the sweet dishes with cardamom, chopped dry fruits, cherries, raisins, cashew, wrapping, pieces of fruits, icing, etc. and the salty dishes with chopped coriander, green chillies, tomato, beetroot, onion rings, carrot, flowers of radish, mint leaves, etc., They will enhance the pleasure of eating and look very interesting.

Great stress has been laid in this book on the decoration aspect, encouraging girls and boys to learn this art along with the culinary art. Provide proper cutlery for serving preparations decorated with spices, dry fruits, etc., like tongs to hold, serving spoon, small spoon, fork, spatula, etc. Put them in order and do concentrate on other things also, like decorating candles, Ikebana, money plant, some show pieces appropriate for the occasion.

The most important aspect is to make a habit of using this art and developing it by giving a new shape to it every day with the help of your novel ideas and experiments.

Tip off
It is said we first eat with our eyes then with the nose and finally with our tongue and teeth.

- If an oven is not available, bake on coal fire. Place big burning pieces of coal in the lower section of the burner (angeethee). Put a tin sheet or a lid on top of the burner. Place a cake tin on it. Put a vessel up-side down on the cake tin and put a few burning pieces of coal on it. Cake will be baked just as in an oven.

- While roasting in an oven, place the food stuff in a vessel with one inch high sides. Gravy will not spill from this vessel. While frying meat, fill three-fourths of a bowl with water and place it in the oven. This will prevent meat from burning and ensure proper cooking.

- While shopping for good quality meat, fish and chicken, keep the following in mind. Fresh meat of goat or lamb will have firm and white fat. While the colour of tender meat will be a mixture of blue and pink and the broken bone in it will be of white colour. Old animal's meat will be a mixture of dark blue and pink and edge of a bone will be red. Do not buy light mauve coloured meat with yellow fat. It is generally stale. If a bird is healthy, its chest should be firm with soft edges of bone. Infirm chest and hard edges of bone belong to an old bird. Fresh fish has life like bright eyes and it smells good. Fish with socketed dead eyes is stale. Its smell is also different.

- To test the freshness of an egg, put it in a vessel with water. If it is fresh, it will remain there in a slanting position. Rotten eggs stand erect in water. If the egg has gone absolutely bad, it will stand erect on its pointed end on the surface of the vessel.

- Fruits and vegetables reveal themselves by touch and smell. Do not buy half ripe, overripe and spoiled fruits. Do not buy off season vegetables and also whithered or broken vegetables and fruits. If the vegetables are to be stored for a long time without refrigeration, wet them and wrap them in a sheet of paper. Fold the paper from all sides, preventing the passage of air through the vegetables. Fruits remain fresh for a longer time, if its stem is coated with wax.

- While buying canned food stuff, see to it that the can is not dented or swollen from any side.

- If a broken egg is to be poached in boiling water, add a spoon of vinegar in the water. This will keep the egg in shape.

- Before making an omelette, brush the frying pan with a pinch of salt, then put the ghee, oil or butter.

- Before beating an egg in a bowl, wet it a bit. The egg won't stick to the bowl. Before extracting juice from a lime, soak it in hot water for a while. The quantity of juice will be more.

- While cooking rice, add a few drops of lime juice to it. Rice will be whiter with separated grains.

- Add a few drops of lime juice while cooking apples also. This will prevent the apples from turning black.

- Boil water before boiling vegetables. Then gradually add vegetables to it in small quantities.

- A pinch of salt added to the water preserves the natural colouring of these vegetables. Root vegetables should be cooked in a closed vessel, on low fire, while green vegetables should be cooked in an open vessel.

- Add piece of cottage cheese (paneer) to onion soup for better taste.

- If the eggs get overboiled leave them in cold water before peeling.

- If a vegetable preparation becomes too salty, make a small ball out of the wheat dough, soak it in the gravy and remove. If the dish becomes too hot with chillies, add a few drops of lime juice to it. Care should be taken to check on all these before serving the food.

- If the juice of a lime or any other citrus fruit is to be added to any milk preparation for taste, add it drop by drop. This will prevent milk from curdling.

- If deeper red colour is preferred for gravy, do not add too much chillie, but take out the seeds from two whole red chillies, soak them in water for half an hour, add a little vinegar to it, squeeze the chillies and add this water to the gravy. The colour will be deep red.

- If hard raw meat is to be made tender, rub lime on it, or wrap it up in banana leaves.

- If bread gets dry, steam it for some time.

- Add more oil and less vinegar to a salad dressing and mix well.

- Add sour flavouring to vegetables only when they are three-fourth cooked, not earlier.

- If ghee is to be added to pastries in place of butter, let it cool before adding the ghee.

- Fried things should be placed on absorbent paper before transferring them on a serving plate or dish.

Tip off

The Menu should be planned for your family as well as for your guests beforehand. If you haven't been following this, try and cultivate this habit for your family as well.

The dining table should be used for family bonding, not for crossing swords over unappetizing dishes.

Your family's daily menu should be planned according to your family members' tastes, their health and needs of individual members. Hard and fast rules cannot be laid down for daily eating, as for special and formal occasions. Neither can the food habits of the family be altered completely. Even then a few general tips should be kept in mind.

Plan lunch, dinner, breakfast and evening tea in such a way that they provide all the nutrition necessary for a day. At the same time, they should not be monotonous. All the meals should have variety. They should be good to eat and balanced too.

Offer Variety

To keep this balance, try to alter the menu every day. Whole week's diet should be balanced in such a way that it provides all that a body needs and at the same time pleases every member of the family by its variety. Choice and necessity of children, adults, women, men, elders, etc. should be incorporated in your menu.

Include one dry and one dish with gravy in the daily menu. If one is heavy, the other should be easily digestible. If one is soft the other should be chewable. That is absolutely essential to activate your teeth. One meal in a day should be simple and light. The other meal could be a little heavy and elaborate. This depends on the convenience of the family. Those going to school, college and office should eat a light lunch and their dinner could be heavier. But it should not be taken too late at night. Those used to taking dinner late should keep it light and lunch could be a full meal. By and large, it is better to follow this rule for a healthy living. Exceptions of course, could be there once in a while.

Make it a habit to serve food in an attractive way. Special decors could be used for special occasions. But the family should not be neglected also. As far as serving of food is concerned, cleanliness and nutrition go with health. Similarly, the art of presenting food plays an important part in mental happiness. Good food not served in an attractive manner will kill the appetite and even if the food is not good and tasty but presented in a pleasant way will enhance your appetite. The joy of eating well served food has its effect on the digestive system.

Serve Well

If you want that family members should give up fried, spicy food and take to dishes that are healthy but less palatable, like salads, you have to give special attention to the art of serving. Clean, presentable serving bowls, shining plates, well presented food on these plates, their colour coordination, flower arrangement on the table, properly laid napkins, spoons, etc. and a smiling face of the hostess will certainly attract everybody towards the dining table. Learn new methods of serving and decorating and keep changing them as you learn new recipes. Your will win everybody's heart and it will help the atmosphere at home remain fresh and lively. Just try it out.

On a holiday, plan one menu like a family feast. Satisfaction, taste and enjoyment should be given priority with of course, healthy food items, such as vegetables and fruits. The meal can be enjoyed together in this way as the joy of a family lunch/dinner has its own part to play in building up your health and keeping you happy.

Tip off

A family that eats healthy food together stays together and remains healthy and cheerful.

*G*uests are welcome in every home. Extending hospitality to the guests is a distinctive part of the great Indian tradition. With changing social and economic conditions, this particular tradition has become a little obscure no doubt, but it has not been wiped out completely, as it happens to be an integral part of our lives.

Adjustments within the existing conditions is a special quality found in most of the Indians. On one hand, they have coped with problems like inflation, scarcity and non-availability of food stuffs and on the other hand, they have incorporated different kinds of delicacies from various states within the country and abroad also, in their eating. With this, there have been remarkable changes in their eating habits and modes of serving food. The adjustments to bring about these changes have indeed been wonderful.

Indian Hospitality

How much labour, money and time is to be spent on looking after the guests depends entirely on the household budget and also the time in hand for a working or stay at home housewife. But *hospitality is a must for every household*. A point worth mentioning here is that though the labour, time and money saving devices are indeed highly developed yet at the same time more attention is being paid to learning special food preparations and to present them in an attractive fashion. All women's magazines carry columns on cookery and young girls show genuine interest in joining cookery classes. The younger generation not only learns to make new food preparations through these cookery columns and classes, but also the art of serving them, and get trained in throwing parties on their own. Such training has been accepted as a part of modern living.

So it is evident that the Indian hospitality has not deteriorated, in spite of many circumstantial setbacks. It has only been moulded according to times, with the help of science and technology. Whether the guests come unannounced or they are invitees on a special occasion; whether the meeting is in a club or a restaurant, or at a specially arranged party, every young lady these days has to know the art of entertaining.

The training imparted in this art may be divided into four parts:

➤ Food cooked should be clean, proper and tasty.
➤ Family's daily necessities and tastes should be taken care of.
➤ As a guest, proper etiquette should be maintained.
➤ Be pleasant as a hostess.

*I*f you do not live in a village and are a part of the urban population, your social sphere is bound to be wide. You may not be visiting clubs, restaurants and parties frequently. But even if you participate in joint functions, parties, some etiquettes and manners have to be observed there too. Lack of knowledge about these may cause embarrassment and create inferiority complex. So it will be advantageous to know the modes of eating-drinking, and conducting oneself on such occasions.

Mixed Culture

Being Indians, we should be proud of our traditions in eating and behaving and we should adopt them in our personal lives. But while mingling with the mixed culture of modern living, it would be in place to conduct oneself according to time, place and atmosphere. For example, if you do not like to use fork and knife for eating, you may keep them aside and eat with your fingers. But if others around are using forks and knives and you would like to be at par with them, you should know the correct way of using forks and knives, otherwise you may become a laughing stock by imitating others in a wrong way. If you are a little watchful, you can get on to the right way by observing others. But it is always better to learn table manners beforehand and learn the etiquette before going to a modern party. Few important tips are given below for your convenience:

➤ When invited to a party, reach there 10 to 15 minutes earlier than the scheduled time. Your reaching too early may cause inconvenience to the host and reaching late will keep others waiting.

➤ If unable to accept an invitation, do inform on the telephone or by writing. Do not forget to thank them for the invitation.

➤ Reach the dining table when requested by the host, not earlier. Your chair should not be too far from the table, or too close to it.

➤ After sitting, unfold the folded or flower like arranged napkin and spread it across your knees to prevent soiling of clothes. This napkin can also be used for wiping hands and mouth.

➤ Do not sit on the chair in a stiff, upright position or bend too much over the table. Do not rest your elbows on the table.

- ➤ Take part in the discussions going on around you, only if you have a thorough knowledge of the subject. Otherwise just be a silent listener, so that it may not occur to others that everything is Greek to you. It is not good to express nervousness or seem indifferent at such moments. In case you have to attend such parties frequently, the best thing to do would be to increase your general knowledge and try and gain popularity on such occasions. Otherwise be in a pleasant mood, behave and show the good aspects of your nature.

- ➤ Learn to use fork and knife beforehand or by observing then and there. Handles of your fork and knife should rest on your palms. Press the food with fork and cut it into small bits with the knife. Your knife should be in the right hand and fork in the left. Put the small pieces of food into your mouth with the fork. While pressing the food, the posterior of your knife should be on a higher level. While putting the morsel into the mouth, the lower part should be higher. It will be easier to slice the food if the elbows are kept close to the body.

- ➤ In a Western meal, soup is served first. A large spoon is provided separately for drinking soup. Soup is to be drunk not from the pointed side of the spoon, but from its sides. Do not make a noise while drinking. Remember, soup is not served again, so do not ask for a second helping.

- ➤ If you need another helping of any preparation, shift your plate a little in front and give an indication to the bearer. Keep in mind that you will be served from your left side. So when the bearer is on your right, he comes to serve the person sitting on your right.

- ➤ If you do not like a preparation, avoid taking it. But do not let others know about your dislikes. May be they are liking it and you may spoil their tastes.

- ➤ If you want to spit out something put the spoon close to your mouth and take it out on the spoon and keep it on one side of your plate. If something seems unpalatable in the food, leave it in the plate without commenting on it. Your speaking about it may spoil other people's mood.

- ➤ If the spoon, knife or fork falls on the ground do not pick it up, but ask the bearer to get you another one, or take one from those kept in a corner of the table.

- ➤ Do not sip tea from the platter. Drink it from the cup. Let the spoon rest on the plate. Do not make a noise while drinking tea or water.

- ➤ Do not speak with food in your mouth, or laugh loudly while eating. While talking to the person next to you, turn only your neck and not the entire body or chair.

➤ Spoon, knife and fork should not bang against your plate, creating loud noise.

➤ If finger bowls with warm water and lime pieces are provided after the meal, use it for cleaning your fingers. Otherwise go and wash your mouth and hands at the place provided for it. If something gets stuck in between the teeth, use a toothpick to remove it. Keep your left hand in front of your mouth while doing this. If there is no arrangement for washing hands, wipe your mouth with the napkin quietly. Before leaving the table, wait for others too, and don't rush to get out.

➤ In the buffet style of eating, lots of formalities are overlooked. Eatables are kept in large bowls on the table and empty plates and spoons, etc. are put along with them. Pick up the plate and the spoon yourself and serve yourself anything you want, as much as you want. Then come away from the table. Sit and eat if chairs are provided, otherwise eat standing. But do not be totally engrossed in eating. Give importance to meeting people. In a buffet meal, you can move about here and there with the plate in your hand and give company to people you know, while eating.

Tip off

Before leaving, it is most important to praise the food. Speak about the lovely décor in front of your host. Tell him about the good time you had. This is more important than just thanking him. Making complaints or talking of unpleasant things on such occasions are taken as bad manners. If you have something adverse on your mind, do not go to the party. Excuse yourself on some pretext or the other.

*J*f you host a function or a formal party at home, extensive preparations are necessary. Cooking, arranging the house, cleaning, decorating and grooming one self-everything has to be done. To top it all, mounting expenses force the hostess to juggle with her budget.

But nothing can be achieved by showing nervousness, creating a lot of noise and keeping other members of the family on their tenterhooks. Things done in confusion are bound to be full of errors, leading to loss of things and also of time. All this will reflect the immaturity of your mind. On the other hand, things done peacefully, in a planned way, taking care of the budget, etc. will show good results, like everything being done in time, in a proper fashion.

You have to be presentable when the guests arrive.

Your house also has to be in order and neat and clean. It is not possible to achieve all this on the day of the party. A few things can be done a day or two in advance. Some things have to be done the same day. Likewise, some chores have to be done well before the party and others are to be accomplished at the last moment. So make a plan of all that you have to do. Place them in order of priority. Few suggestions are given below for your convenience:

➤ Shampoo your hair one or two days before the party, so that they can be set properly on that day. Washing, shopping and other such chores should be done a day or two in advance, so that no pending work remains to be done on that day.

➤ An evening before the party make a trip to your beautician for facial, pedicure, manicure, etc. Take a long bath well before the party. File your nails and shape your eyebrows also. This will save time to get dressed just before the party and it will also help you to feel and look fresh.

➤ Have a glass of fresh lime in the morning and take a light meal, so that you do not feel sluggish after eating and have enough energy to cope with the work. Brush you teeth thoroughly in the morning.

➤ Choose the dress you will be wearing in the evening and hang it at the proper place. Children's clothes and socks, etc. should also be conveniently placed, so that no time is wasted looking for them.

HOSTING A PARTY

➤ Because you will work in the kitchen till late, do not use make-up too early. Complete you work in the kitchen, clean and arrange your house and then devote the last hour to yourself. Use light make-up an hour before the guests arrive.

➤ Do up yourself and also your house well before the party. Decorate your living room and also the entrance of the house. Rangoli designs, an ethnic pot, wall hangings, Ikebana in a corner, drift wood arrangement, all these will give a special look to the entrance. If it is not possible to use any of these, arrange the flower pots in a special way – in groups or in rows. Flower arrangements on the dining table should be done in the evening.

➤ If you have a fridge, make a few dishes the previous day and store in the refrigerator. Vegetables, soup, hot snacks, cutlets, *vadas*, etc. should be made fresh on the same day. If the weather is not too hot, a few things can be made earlier, even if there is no facility for storing them in a refrigerator. A few things like desserts, can be bought also, or sweet dish like 'Ras Malai' can be made on the same day in the morning. Fried things like *pakodas* should be freshly made and served hot.

➤ Some of the fried things like *kachori*, *pakodi*, etc. can be fried earlier and heated up again in ghee before serving. *Bhature-chhole* also can be made earlier and heated up before eating. Things like *puris* and *dosas* should be made absolutely fresh. If you do not have any help for such last moment's chores, hire somebody for that evening, or take the help of a friend or neighbour. Only then you will have time to pay attention to your guests.

➤ If you do not have any help avoid inviting too many people at a time. Call them for tea instead of a meal. Even then, more than fifteen or twenty guests together may create confusion, especially when the place is small. A small place crowded with too many people is inconvenient for the host and for the guests as well.

➤ In case you have enough space and a few invitees and two or three people to help you, you may arrange small tables for a tea party or a dinner. Put chairs around these tables, (such parties are more enjoyable outdoors in a garden) or put one single long table, (two tables may be combined to make a large one). Place chairs all around and decorate the table nicely. A bouquet of flowers or ikebana flower arrangement can be placed in the centre. There should be a table mat on the table in front of each chair and plates, spoons, knives, forks and glasses should be placed properly on them. Spread bigger mats in the centre of the table with enough room for serving bowls. Extra things like utensils, plates, etc. should be put on a separate table nerarby, to avoid going to the kitchen repeatedly.

➤ A hot plate, to warm up food, can be placed on this additional table. Plates for desserts can be

placed and arrangements for betel leaves to be taken after meal can also be made on this table. (More details on table decoration given in the following pages.)

➤ If eating is to be in Western style, do not request your guests to eat more. This has to be borne in mind all the time.

➤ Join your guests for the meal, but commence eating with them and not before. Keep your guests company during the meal. Do not finish eating first. This can be embarrassing for your guests and they may hesitate to take fresh helpings.

➤ Keep the atmosphere light and cheerful during the meal. If by chance a mild tiff comes up between two people, try to divert the topic, avoiding offence to any of the guests. Light musical entertainment or mimicry, etc. can be arranged on such occasions.

➤ Lastly, another important thing to be remembered. It very often happens that the hostess looks very presentable. Living and dining rooms, *verandah*, outside, etc. are spick and span, but due to pressure of work, the cleanliness and orderliness of bathroom, kitchen, etc. is thoroughly neglected. This is not right. If any of your guests need to use the bathroom or somebody (specially women) are keen to have peep inside the house, it will not create a good impression. All your outside decoration will seem dull and drab then. Do not show your inefficiency in this manner. After being through with your work, clean up and arrange the kitchen – in fact, the whole house. Ask your domestic help to have a wash after work, wear clean clothes and be ready before the guests arrive.

➤ Guests will praise you after the party and you will apologise for your little shortcomings, politely. Do not mention the hard work you have put in or the tensions you have gone through to make the party a success.

*I*f your place is small and help is lacking, but at the same time, it is essential to host a dinner or a lunch, arrange a 'buffet' meal. That will be convenient for you. All the food is served in big bowls on one table for everybody to eat together. Full plates and spoons, etc. are placed separately. Guests will stand around the table, pick up their own plates and spoons and serve themselves whatever they want to eat. There is less wastage of food like this and serving everybody individually can also be avoided.

In a 'buffet', you have to pay attention to the following things.

➤ See that the table cloth is spotlessly clean.

➤ Serving bowls should be absolutely clean and sparkling.

➤ Put appropriate serving spoon with every dish on the table.

➤ The food should be hot.

➤ Small bowls or soup plates can be put separately for curd or dessert.

➤ Keep a few empty plates for peeled skin of fruits.

➤ Place one napkin with each plate.

➤ In a buffet meal, paper napkins should be used, to be thrown away later.

➤ Water jug and glasses should be placed on a separate table.

➤ Arrangement should be made for washing hands.

➤ If coffee or tea is to be served, give it hot after the meal – either on the same table or on a separate one, as convenient.

This way of entertaining will be less troublesome for you and your guests will also feel free. But you have to go, find and see to it that all the invitees have eaten well. Pay attention to everybody alike and a little more to those who for some reason had joined others at the table, later.

If there is ample space, rows of chairs can be put a little away from the table, on a side. These chairs can be used by those who prefer to sit and eat. If there is lack of space, people can stand and eat. Soft music in the background helps to make the atmosphere lively.

*Y*ou do invite your child's friends on his or her birthday. It is an occasion to light candles on a cake, cut it with the strains of 'Happy birthday to you'. You can think of some new ideas, different from the mixed traditions of India and the West. Here are some suggestions for your consideration.

Invite elders only if the child is very small. As soon as they understand the significance of a birthday, invite children of their age group, their friends, so that they feel free to enjoy themselves without the presence of elders. You may include your neighbour's children, even if they are a little younger or older than your child. There will be two gains thus – children in the family and neighbourhood will not feel neglected and secondly, children will not remain confined to their own age group only, but will learn to mix with the younger and older children and also to behave socially. Games to be played before the party can be for the children of the same age group.

Planning the Menu

Your work extends beyond preparing dishes and serving them on each plate for each child. While planning the menu, children's liking must be taken into account. Food should be healthy too. Do not include items like *Chnolekulche, Chaat, Mathha* made of flour, *Balushahi*, etc., Decide on things like sweet toasts, juicy sweets made of dried thickened milk, salty puffed rice, fruit cream of ice cream, salty *pakodis* made of *moong, cake, pastries, biscuits, toffees*, etc. Decorate them nicely and arrange them on the table. To enhance the beauty of the party, a few eatables can be included just for decoration or fun. Bird and cock made of dried thickened milk and a joker made with boiled potatoes can also be included just for decorating the table. Boiled eggs in different shapes can also be arranged. Sweet dishes can be garnished with chopped dry fruits, cherries and salty dishes with chopped coriander leaves, grated cottage cheese (paneer), tomato, sauce, etc., to give the dish a different look.

Decorations

Venue of the party should also be decorated according to the children's liking. Have colourful balloons. Arrange photos, cartoons and toys. Caps can be made with coloured papers, golden strips or *Rakhis* kept at home for the children to wear.

Games

Arrange for some games before eating. Have some programmes that will make them laugh. You may think of some light quiz or competition and keep some small prizes for the winners. But such competitions should not give an inferiority complex to any child on a happy occasion. Nobody should feel insulted or ashamed. This has to be borne in mind all the time. It is better to give gifts like toffees, balloons, small toys, picture books, etc., to all the children and some thing extra for the winners.

The most important thing is that you should not confine yourself to the arrangements of the party, alone. You should also not interfere in their games and other entertainments. If the children are enjoying themselves along with the good food, they will cherish the fun of the party for a long time. Your child will also be happy to know that his/her friends had a lovely time and they went back home with pleasant memories of the party. It is unfair to curb the children with words like: "Children, sit quietly, eat silently, do not make noise, etc." This will spoil their fun and mood of the party, as they have come to enjoy and have fun. So without making any nuisance or spoiling any household items – leave them free to play, talk, sing, eat or drink.

Tip off

Children love games and good food. So give them both aplenty and you've won some little loving friends for life.

PART - II

MOUTH-WATERING RECIPES

Kachori

Almost every festival in North India is celebrated with *kachoris*. They are crispy, tasty and mouth-watering when served hot.

Kachori

Ingredients

¾ cup skinless *urad dal* (black grams)
4 cups flour (atta)
1 or 2 green chillies chopped
salt to taste
oil (for deep frying)
1 tbsp aniseeds (saunf)
1 tsp coriander seeds
½ tsp red chilli powder
¼ tsp asafoetida powder

Method

Soak the *urad dal* (black grams) in water overnight, then rinse and drain. Grind the drained *dal* with the chilli powder, salt and spices to make the stuffing. Mix well and divide it into 16 equal portions. Sift the flour and gradually add enough water to make a soft dough. Cover the dough with damp cloth and leave for about 30 minutes. Divide the dough into 16 round parts, using wet hands, and smear each portion with a little oil. Flatten and roll out into 2 inch round balls. Wrap one portion of stuffing in each round and roll into a smooth ball, using greased hands. Flatten and roll into a 3-4 inch round *chapatti*. Heat plenty of oil in a deep frying pan or a wok (kadhai). Now lift the rolled *kachori* and carefully slip it into the hot oil. Immediately start flickering hot oil over the top of it with a spatula so that it will swell up like a ball. This should take only a few seconds. Flip the *kachori* over and cook the other side until golden brown. Serve the *dal kachori* hot with *chutney* and *aloo sabji* (potato curry).

Tip off

Urad dal (black gram) may be replaced by *moong dal* (green gram) or mashed potatoes, as per your taste and desire.

Samosa

Samosa is a popular snack of North India. It is relished by almost all–rich and poor, small and big, and old and young.

Samosa

Ingredients

For Cover:
1 cup *maida* (white flour)
water (to knead the dough)
2 tbsps of oil
salt (to taste)
¼ tsp *ajwain* or carom seeds (optional)

For Stuffing:
3-4 potatoes (boiled, peeled and mashed)
½ cup green peas (boiled)
1-2 green chillies (finely chopped)
½ tsp ginger (crushed)
1 tbsp coriander (finely chopped)
few chopped cashew nuts (optional)
few raisins (optional)
½ tsp *garam masala*
salt (to taste)
red chilli powder (to taste)
½ tsp *amchoor* (dry mango powder)

Method

Mix all the ingredients (salt, oil, *ajwain* or carom seeds) except water. Add a little water at a time. Pat and knead well for several times into a soft pliable dough. Cover it with moist muslin cloth and keep aside for 15 minutes. In a bowl, add the mashed potatoes and all the dry powdered spices (masalas) (salt, chilli powder, dry mango powder, *garam masala*) and green chillies, ginger and mix well. Add the green peas, cashew nuts and raisins, if you want and mix well. Add the coriander and keep aside. Make small rolls of dough and roll it into a 4"-5" diameter circle. Cut it into two parts like semi-circles. Now take one semi-circle and fold it like a cone. Use water while doing so. Place a spoon of the filling in the cone and seal the third side using a drop of water. Heat oil in a *kadhai* or wok and deep fry on a medium flame till golden brown. Serve the *samosas* hot with green *chutney* and tamarind *chutney*.

Tip off

You may change the filling in the *samosa* and put more vegetables or *paneer* (cottage cheese) in it to make it more nutritious and delicious.

Gujhias

This delicacy is specially prepared during festivals, such as Holi celebrated in almost the entire of North India.

Gujhias

Ingredients

150 gms white flour or *maida*
water (for kneading)
150 gms semolina
125 gms dried thickened milk
125 gms sugar or more
according to the taste
chopped almonds, cashew nuts,
walnuts, raisins, etc, nutmeg, cardamom
seeds, as you desire to garnish

Method

Add two tablespoons of ghee to 150 gms. of white flour or *maida*. Knead, sprinkling cold water. The dough should be a little hard. Leave it covered with a wet piece of cloth.

For the stuffing, roast 125 gms of semolina (suji) in ghee on low fire. When the semolina turns pink, add 125 gms. of dried thickened milk and stir for another three minutes. Now add the chopped almonds, walnuts, cashew nuts, raisins, nutmeg, cardamom seeds and remove from fire. Add 125 gms. of ground sugar or more and keep aside.

Knead the dough again and divide into small balls. Roll like thin, round *puris*. Place the stuffing on one part of the round ball and double it up by wetting the edges. Lift the edges with fingers and shape them in a zig zag or cut the edges with a cutter to give the shape of a *gujhia*. Stuff all the *gujhias* similarly.Then deep fry them in ghee in a vessel or *kadhai* (wok). Flame should be high in the beginning and then it should be lowered to cook them well from outside, as well as inside. Dip these *gujhias* in a thin sugary syrup and take out. Decorate on a plate with silver paper, rose petals and cherries as per your wish.

Tip off

In North India, the *gujhias* are a delicacy during the Holi festival or during other fasts and festivals.

Chhole Bhaturae

Chhole Bhaturae is a delicacy straight from the kitchen of Punjab.

Chhole Bhaturae

Ingredients

250 gms of *kabuli chana* or Bengal gram
2 glasses of water used for soaking
4 onions sliced
8-10 flakes of peeled garlic
1 inch piece of ginger– thinly sliced
salt
red chilli powder
turmeric
¼ tsp of edible soda

Method

For Chhole: Cook the Bengal Gram (kabuli chana) for about 20 to 25 minutes or half an hour in a pressure cooker. The Bengal Grams should be tender but should remain whole. So stir lightly. Water should not evaporate completely or be too much. Now sauté the onion, garlic, ginger, etc. in ghee or oil and then add the *chole*. Garnish with *garam masala* and coriander leaves. Green chillies can also be decorated on top. Use pounded pomegranate seeds (anaar daana) dried mango powder (amchur) or lemon juice for a little sour taste.

For Bhaturae: Mix about two cups of white flour (maida) and 1 cup of fine semolina (suji) for the *Bhaturae*. Soak them in a cup of sour curd overnight, or mix readymade yeast and knead after an hour. If the dough puffs up one and half times more, it is ready for the *Bhaturae*. Rub a little ghee or oil on your palms and knead this flour making balls a little larger than for the *puris*. Roll them with both hands into thin round *puris* and deep fry them in a pan or *kadhai* (wok). Keep the flame high to begin with, but lower it immediately after putting in the *bhaturae* in ghee. Take out when light red in colour. These *Bhaturae* are to be served with spicy sour *Chole*.

Tip off

Tie tea leaves in a small piece of cloth and boil them along with the Bengal grams. Tea leaves give the dark chocolate colour to the grams.

Masala Dosa

Masala Dosa is liked by people all over the world, but it is basically a delicacy of South India.

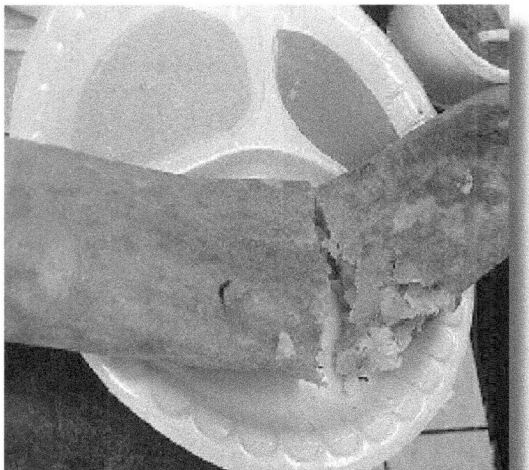

Masala Dosa

Ingredients

2 cups rice
1 cup *urad dal* (black gram)
2 boiled potatoes
1 or 2 onions (chopped)
1 or 2 tomatoes (chopped)
red chilli powder or green chillies as per your taste

Method

Soak two cups of rice and one cup of *urad dal* (black grams) separately for six to eight hours. Grind them separately and mix them. The consistency of the batter should be thick. Make a filling by frying the boiled potatoes, onions and tomatoes together. Heat the ghee or oil on *tawa* or non-stick frying pan with a thick bottom. Put a spoon of batter in the middle and spread it in round shape with a spoon till it is thin. Put ghee on the sides also, so that the *dosa* does not stick to the *tawa*. Put the potato and tomato filling in it. When crisp and cooked, fold into two. Serve the dosa with coconut *chutney* and sambhar or only with *chutney*.

To make the Sambhar: Cook small pieces of brinjal, potatoes, beans (sem) and cauliflower, etc., in *Arhar dal*. When *dal* is half-cooked, add tamarind water and cook again in a cooker. Add salt and Sambhar powder during cooking. Temper with asafoetida, mustard seeds, fenugreek and garnish with curry leaves. The consistency should be thin.

For the Coconut *Chutney*: Grate the raw coconut. Heat oil and fry the grated coconut along with chopped green chillies and curry leaves (meetha neem). Bring down from the fire and grind, adding tamarind, salt and ginger.

Tip off

Plain Dosa (without filling) is served with *Sambhar* and Masala dosa (with filling) is served with *Chutney*. But both may also be used and served together.

Idli

Soft and fluffy idlis are tasty and easily digestible.

Idli

Ingredients

2 cups rice
1 cup skinless *urad dal* (black grams)
1½ tbsp of salt
a pinch of baking soda
oil or ghee or butter (for greasing)

Method

Pick, wash and soak the *dal* and rice separately overnight or for eight to ten hours. Grind the rice coarsely in a blender. Grind the *dal* into a smooth and frothy paste. Now mix the grinded rice and *dal* together into a batter. Mix salt and set aside in a warm place overnight for fermenting. Idlis are ready to be cooked when the batter is well fermented. Grease the idli holder or pan well and fill each of them with 3/4th full of batter. Steam the cook the idlis on medium flame for about 10 minutes or until done. Use a butter knife to remove the idlis. Serve them with *sambhar* and coconut *chutney*.

Tip off

To make Rawa Idli, use *sooji* (semolina) instead of rice and *dal*. This idli is easy to make and is delicious too!

Upma

Upma is a healthy snack which can be fed to small children also. It can be prepared in different ways, with or without vegetables. However, with fresh cooked vegetables, it is really yummy!

Upma

Ingredients

1 cup rava/*sooji* (semolina)
25 gms fried cashew nuts (optional)
1 inch ginger (chopped)
1 or 2 chopped onions
3 green chillies (slit sideways)
1 or 2 potatoes (chopped)
1 capsicum (chopped)
1 carrot (chopped)
chopped pieces of cauliflower
1/4 cup green peas frozen or fresh
1 tsp mustard seeds
1 tsp *urad dal* (black gram)
1 tsp *chana dal* (brown chick peas)
salt (to taste)
½ tsp turmeric powder
chilli powder (to taste) (optional)
2 tbsp oil or ghee
few curry leaves
finely chopped coriander leaves
1 tbsp ghee or oil
lemon juice (to taste)

Method

Sift the *rava* or *sooji* or the semolina through a muslin / cheese cloth or very fine sieve. Heat the ghee in a *kadahi* or wok and fry rava on a moderate heat, stirring constantly to a light brown colour and set aside. Now heat two tbsp of oil in a pan and add the mustard seeds allowing them to splatter. Add the *channa* and *urad dals* and curry leaves to it and fry till they turn red. Add the onions, ginger and green chillies. Sauté for 2-3 minutes. Add all the vegetables, turmeric, chilli powder, and salt to taste. Now add three cups of water and cover the pan allowing it to simmer on low heat until the vegetables are done. Add the fried *rava* to it stirring constantly till it becomes little thick. Take off from the fire and add the lemon juice. Serve it hot garnished with cashew nuts and coriander.

Tip off

Upma is a light, nutritious snack which is low in calories and tasty as well.

Vada

Hot, crisp vadas can be eaten any time of the day. They are a treat with tea and coffee.

Vada

Ingredients

½ cup *urad dal* (black grams)
½ cup rice
1 or 2 onions (finely chopped)
1 tsp ginger
1-2 green chillies (finely chopped)
salt (to taste)
¼ tsp baking soda

Method

Pick, wash and soak the *urad dal* (black gram) and rice for three or four hours. Grind them coarsely in a blender. Now add the onions, ginger, green chillies and salt as per taste along with baking powder. Then mix well. Set aside for about five to ten minutes. Heat oil or ghee in a pan or *kadhai* (wok) and deep fry a spoonful of batter till golden brown giving it a round shape. Serve it hot with tomato sauce, coconut *chutney* or *sambhar*.

Tip off

You may serve the vadas with *chutney* or *sambhar* as breakfast or as a tea time snack.

Rasogullas

Soft, spongy rasogullas of Kolkata are famous all over the world.

Rasogullas

Ingredients

1 kg milk
juice of lemon
2 tsps of semolina
some sugar candy (mishris)
375 gms sugar
1 tsp rose water (optional)

Method

Prepare about 250 gms of cottage cheese (paneer) by curdling milk with drops of lemon juice. Add two spoons of semolina and knead well. Divide this mixture into 15-16 small round balls. A small piece of sugar candy (mishri) should be placed in the middle of each ball. Now make thin syrup with 375 gms of sugar. Divide this syrup into two portions. Gradually put the balls into half of the syrup and let it cook till it dries up. Then put these balls in the other half of the syrup and let it cool. Sprinkle rose water, if you like and serve.

Tip off

To make yellow rasogullas, add saffron or yellow food colour to the mixture. It is also called Rajbhog. The Rajbhog is prepared slightly bigger than the Rasogullas in Bengal.

Momos

Momos are also known as *samosas of East India*.

Momos

Ingredients

1 cup refined white flour (maida)
French beans, finely chopped
1 medium sized carrot, finely chopped
4-5 fresh button mushrooms (finely chopped)
2 spring onions, finely chopped
¼ cup bean sprouts
8-10 chopped cashewnuts
ginger (finely chopped)
green chilli (finely chopped)
8-10 black peppercorns (crushed)
½ tbsp light soya sauce
1 tsp sesame oil (til oil)
salt (to taste)
spring onions (chopped)

Method

Mix the *maida* (white flour) with five tablespoons of water and knead into a stiff dough. Cover with a damp cloth and set aside for 15-20 minutes. For the filling, combine the French beans, carrots, mushrooms, spring onions, bean sprouts, cashew nuts, ginger, green chillies, peppercorns, soya sauce, sesame oil and salt in a large bowl. Divide the dough into sixteen equal round portions and roll into small thin discs. Place a spoonful of the vegetable filling or boiled minced meat filling in the centre of each disc and bring the sides together in the centre, pinching firmly together to form a dumpling. Line a steamer rack with a clean, damp piece of muslin and arrange the momos on it. Place the rack in the steamer, cover and steam for 8-10 minutes until the momos are cooked through. Transfer to a serving plate. Garnish with spring onion greens and serve hot with *Sichuan Sauce*. The *Sichuan Sauce* is a Chinese Sauce, easily available in the markets.

Tip off

To make non-vegetarian momos, substitute the vegetarian filling with minced and boiled chicken or mutton filling. You can also use minced cottage cheese (paneer) as a filling.

Sandesh

Sandesh is a speciality of West Bengal. It is very light and tasty as no oil or frying is involved in its cooking.

Sandesh

Ingredients

225 or 250 gms *paneer* or cottage cheese
150 to 200 gms sugar
1 tbsp rose water (optional)
½ tsp green cardamom seeds (grounded)

Method

Combine the sugar and the cottage cheese (paneer) and mix well. Place the mixture over the heat and stir constantly to avoid lumps. When the mixture solidifies, splash the rose water on it, if you like and remove the frying pan from the heat. Stir for few more times. Place the cardamom in a separate plate Now divide the mixture into several portions of the required size and flatten them to give the desired shapes. Dip each piece into the plate of cardamoms and biscuit crumbs so that the front of the *sandesh* is coated with crumbs. Serve the *sandesh* cold.

Tip off

Refrigerate the Sandesh soon after they are ready because the *paneer* or cottage cheese does not stay fresh at room temperature for long.

Fish Curry

In Bengal, the fish curry is eaten with rice. It is the staple food of Bengal.

Fish Curry

Ingredients

8 fish fillets or pieces
2 tbsps lemon juice
mustard oil (for frying)
salt (to taste)
1 tbsp red chilli powder
4 red chillies (whole)
1 tsp mustard paste
1 tsp turmeric powder
4 green chillies (slit or chopped)
2 tbsps of coriander powder
1 tbsp garlic paste
1 tsp mustard seeds
1 bay leaf
2 cups of onions (chopped)
1 tbsp ginger paste
1 tsp turmeric powder
1 tsp onion seeds (kalonji)

Method

Clean and cut the fish fillets further, if you like, wash well, remove excess water and then marinate with lime juice, turmeric powder and salt. Keep aside for about 30 minutes. Heat up a frying pan, mix in 1 tbsp oil, shallow fry marinated fish from both sides until slightly browned. Take off and keep aside. Heat up the remaining oil, mix in mustard seeds, *kalonji*, whole dry red chillies and bay leaf. Stir fry for a few minutes till seeds crackle. Mix in ginger, garlic paste and stir fry again for a moment. Mix in cut onions and stir fry until slightly brown in colour. Mix in the mustard paste, red chilli powder, coriander powder and turmeric powder. Stir fry the *masala* (spices) nicely until the oil starts separating. Adjust the water and salt, bring to boil and then mix in the shallow fried fish. Put the green chillies slits on top. Stir fry on a slow flame until the fish gets cooked and the oil starts floating on top of the gravy. Decorate with cut green coriander leaves.

Tip off

In the fish curry, poppy seed paste may also be added to give it a special flavour.

Poha

Poha is made of rice, hence it is considered a light snack. However, it is quite nutritious and healthy for children and adults both.

Poha

Ingredients

2 cups fine *poha*
sliced onions
boiled potatoes
½ cup boiled peas
pinch of asafoetida
¼ tsp mustard seeds
curry leaves
chopped green chillies, turmeric
salt (to taste)
grated coconut and coriander (to garnish)

Method

Clean about two cups of beaten rice (pohe or chewra) and wash. Soak in half a cup of water for ten minutes. Heat oil or ghee in a vessel and put the asafoetida and mustard seeds. Add the sliced onions and potato rings or peas and fry on low heat till cooked with a red or light brown colour. Put the curry leaves, chopped green chillies and the turmeric paste or powder. By this time, soaked beaten rice will get puffed up. Put them in the vessel and add one spoon of sugar and salt according to taste. Stir lightly and leave it covered on low fire for three to four minutes. Remove on a plate and garnish with chopped coriander leaves and grated coconut.

Tip off

Poha or *Chewra*, of coarser variety, is soaked in water for a longer period than of the fine variety.

Khaman Dhokla

Khaman dhoklas are famous as special Gujarati snacks. They are also very light, healthy and tasty.

Ingredients

250 gms *besan* (gram flour)
2 cups of sour buttermilk
¼ tsp backing soda,
salt (to taste)
pinch of asafoetida
¼ tsp mustard seeds
1 tsp oil
sliced tomatoes and
green chillies (to garnish)

Khaman Dhokla

Method

Soak about 250 gms coarsely ground gram flour (besan) in two cups of sour buttermilk. Then according to the weather, leave it for 24 to 36 hours, till it puffs to double. Now whip adding ¼ spoon of soda and salt according to taste. Mixture should not be too thin and should have a cream like consistency. Spread it on a greased plate with high sides and cook in steam. If it is to be cooked in the cooker, put the mixture in a vessel with a tight lid, or put water in a big vessel and place a bowl on it. Put the plate of mixture on the bowl and cover it with a lid. Place some weight on the lid. Open after 15 minutes and check with a knife. If the mixture does not stick to the knife, it is done. Remove from fire and cut into pieces. Spread the tempering of asafoetida and mustard seeds fried in oil or ghee on the top. Decorate on a plate with tomato and green chillies.

Tip off

Dhokla can also be made with *sooji* (semolina). It is easily digestible. Just use *sooji* in place of *besan* (gram flour).

Bhelpuri

Bhelpuri is a famous and popular dish of Mumbai.

Bhelpuri

Ingredients

1 cup puffed rice
small fried rounds of wheat
flour as used in *chaat*
pieces of boiled potato
fried rings of potato
salted strings (bhujiya, sev) of
gram flour (besan)

Method

Mix the above mentioned ingredients and add one finely chopped onion, chopped green chillies, salt, black salt, fried ground cumin seeds, black pepper as per taste to the mixture and mix well. Sprinkle one spoon of mint (pudina) sauce. Mix well and serve like the popular *chaat* of North India.

Tip off

These days ready to eat packed packets of Bhelpuri are available in the market. Just open the packet and mix everything. Your instant bhelpuri is ready to eat!

Khandvi

Khandvi is also a snack of Gujarat, soft and succulent in taste.

Khandvi

Ingredients

½ cup *besan* (gram flour)
1 cup thin buttermilk
salt (to taste)
2-3 pinches of turmeric powder
1 tbsp oil
1 tsp sesame seeds
½ tsp mustard seeds
1 tbsp coconut (scraped)
1 tbsp coriander (finely chopped)
2 pinches asafoetida
2 green chillies (finely chopped)
1 stalk curry leaves

Method

Mix water, *besan* (gram flour), salt and turmeric to form a batter. Heat the oil in a heavy frying pan, and then add the batter. Stir vigorously and evenly to avoid lump formation. Cook till the mixture does not taste raw, stirring continuously. When done (about 7-8 minutes), pour a ladleful in a large plate. Spread as thin as possible with the back of a large flat spoon. Use circular outward movements as for the *dosas*. When cool, cut into 2" wide strips. Carefully roll each strip, repeat for all the plates. Place them in a serving dish. Sprinkle coconut and coriander all over the *khandvi* rolls. Heat oil or ghee in a small frying pan. Add the cumin, asafoetida, curry leaves and chopped green chillies. Add the sesame seeds and immediately pour over the *khandvi* rolls. Serve with garlic *chutney*.

Tip off

The mixture of coconut and other spices should be filled in each piece of *khandvi* to get the right taste.

Italian Pizza

Pizza offers a lot of variety in the form of its toppings.

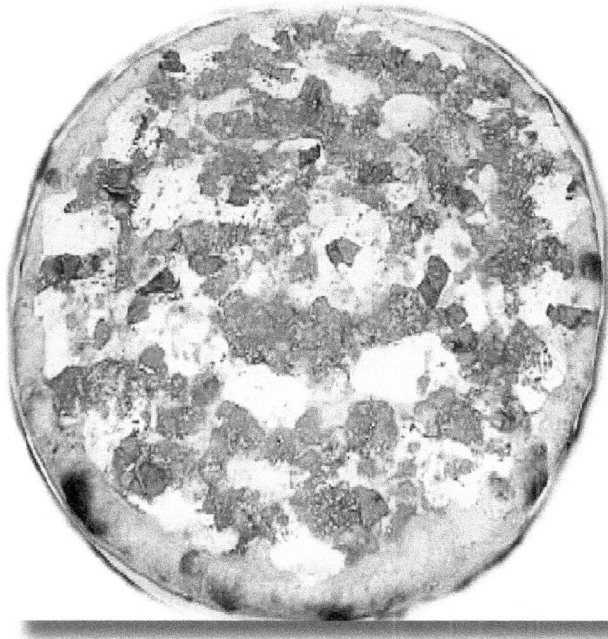
Italian Pizza

Ingredients

225 gms *maida* (white flour)
¼ tsp salt
15 gms yeast mixed with 4-5 tbsps of hot water
1 tbsp sugar
150 ml milk powder
2 tbsps of butter
½ cup tomato sauce
1 packet grated cheese
1 capsicum cut into pieces
2 large onions (cut into rings)
½ tsp salt
½ tsp pepper powder
2 or 3 tbsps butter (melted)

Method

Mix yeast in hot water and leave it to be frosty. In a bowl, put *maida* (white flour), salt, sugar and mix with milk and yeast. Add the butter. Knead until the dough becomes soft and pliable. Leave the dough to rise double in size. Punch into the dough with your hands and knead again to make into equal balls of shape (as big as you want.) Now flatten the dough with a rolling pin. Sprinkle with flour if the dough is sticky. Put the mini round dough in a greased flat baking pan. Brush the mini pizza with tomato sauce. Add in a bit of capsicum pieces in the centre, top with onion rings and grated cheese. Do the same to all the other pizzas. Pre-heat the oven for 180°C and bake for about 15-20 minutes. You can serve with chilli sauce, tomato sauce and mustard.

Tip off

Sprinkle a bit of melted margarine on the pizza to get a crunchy taste.

Pasta

Pasta can be eaten as a snack or as a meal.

Pasta

Ingredients

1 cup mixed pasta (coloured
fussili, penne and farfalle)
½ cup processed cheese (grated)
1 tbsp oil
2 tbsps of butter
2 tbsps whole wheat flour (atta)
2 cups milk or as required
salt (to taste)
white pepper powder (to taste)
½ cup corn kernels (canned)
1 tsp fresh parsley (chopped)

Method

Boil water in a non-stick deep pan with salt and one tablespoon of oil. Add all the pastas and cook till soft, but firm. Drain and keep aside. Heat two tablespoons of butter or oil in a non-stick pan. Add the whole wheat flour and sauté lightly, taking care that it does not change colour. Add the milk, gradually, stirring continuously so that no lumps are formed. Keeping aside two tablespoons of grated cheese, add the rest to the sauce and continue to stir. After adding the cheese, the sauce will thicken further, so add more milk to adjust the consistency. Add salt, white pepper powder and mix. Add the pasta and corn kernels and mix. Sprinkle the reserved cheese and chopped parsley on top and serve.

Tip off

Add three tablespoons of tomato ketchup and one teaspoon of chilli sauce for variation once in a while.

Italian Cannelloni

The Italian cuisine has many dishes prepared with cheese.

Italian Cannelloni

Ingredients

2 cups flour
2 eggs
2 tbsps of ghee or butter
salt (as per taste)
100 gms boiled potatoes
100 gms boiled peas
100 gms boiled carrots
1 big tomato
1 cup boiled macaroni
250 gms mince meat, vegetables
or cottage cheese
3 tsps of tomato sauce
3 tsps of white sauce
2 onions
cottage cheese, black pepper,
green chillies, salt and butter (to taste)

Method

Mix salt, two big spoons of ghee and two eggs with flour and knead into a dough, using ice cold water. Put it away in the fridge or wrap in wet cloth for about one hour. Knead it again. Divide it into twenty round balls.

For filling, boil and mash the potatoes. Grate the carrots. Boil the mince separately and mix. Add the chopped onions, green chillies, coriander leaves, salt and black pepper. Add the boiled macaroni in the end. Now mix tomato sauce.

Boil in a vessel. Roll the *chapattis* out of the four and the egg mixture. Put in boiling water one by one. The *chapatti* will go down first and then float after being cooked. Take out and spread on a greased plate. Put the filling on it. Roll the *chapatti* and fix the two ends with a toothpick. Place them on a buttered baking tray and decorate with some design on the dividing lines. Sprinkle with sauce and finely chopped coriander leaves. Draw lines with butter on top and bake for about 20 minutes in an oven.

Tip off

White sauce can be made with cornflour. It adds to the taste of almost any continental dish.

Chinese American Chopsuey

This sweet and sour crispy Chinese dish is tasty to eat and easy to cook.

Chinese American Chopsuey

Ingredients

½ cup noodles
½ cup chopped cabbage,
carrots, beans, fruits
1 or 2 small tomatoes
1 or 2 small onions
¼ cup prawn
½ chicken pieces
1 or 2 egg
2 tsps of arrowroot
ajinomoto (spice), salt and
refined oil (to taste)

Method

Fry the noodles in oil on low fire. Dip the sliced vegetables in salted boiling water. Add the tomato sauce, ajinomoto and a little salt in this water and cook the chicken pieces and prawns in it. Add the arrowroot while cooking.

In a big plate, put the noodles on one side. On the other side, keep the boiled vegetables with cooked chicken pieces and prawns on top of it, with a fried egg/eggs on top for garnishing. Serve with vinegar and chilli sauce.

Tip off

The crispy taste of chopsuey is quite appealing to the taste buds.

Chinese Special Mix Chowmein

Chowmein are best eaten with chopsticks.

Mix Chowmein

Ingredients

½ or 1 cup noodles
¼ cup Indian beans, cabbage.
carrots and other sliced vegetables
¼ or ½ cup prawns
few pieces of pork/chicken
ajinomoto (spice), salt, oil,
soya sauce (to taste)

Method

Boil the noodles and strain. If fresh noodles are to be made at home, break an egg, mix a little flour and make it into a stiff dough as for the *puris* (water not to be used).

Roll it on a wooden plank with the help of arrowroot like a thin *chapatti*. It should be thinner than a *chapatti* used to make *samosas*. Sprinkle the arrowroot and fold it. Cut long thin pieces from these folds. Steam these pieces for about five minutes or dip them in boiling water. Put them in a pan, sprinkle one spoon of oil on top. Toss them with a fork and separate the noodles. Fresh noodles made at home are tastier. Put the sliced cabbage, carrots and other vegetables in boiling water and take them out half-cooked. Boil the prawns, pork and chicken pieces separately, as per choice. Fry the vegetables in 3 to 4 spoons of oil first and then the chicken or meat pieces. Mix the salt, ajinomoto, soya sauce and noodles with vegetables and meat before serving.

Tip off

Vegetarians can leave out the prawn, pork and chicken pieces, and can add paneer or cottage cheese, instead.

Vegetable Spring Rolls ━━━━━

These are Chinese finger foods. They are eaten as starters in a Chinese meal.

Vegetable Spring Rolls

Ingredients

1 tbsp flour
1 or 2 eggs
1 tbsp of arrowroot
cabbage, carrots, beans, onions
and other sliced vegetables
salt, ajinomoto
(spice) and oil (to taste)

Method

Mix the eggs and flour. Sprinkle the arrowroot and add the salt and water to make a batter of thin consistency. Heat the oil in a frying pan and spread this batter as done to make the pancakes. Fry both sides and keep aside. Cut the vegetables finely. Grate the onions and carrots. Fry the vegetables in oil. Put salt and ajinomoto. Spread the fried pancakes and place the sliced vegetables on it. Roll it. Double up both the edges and stick them together with the whipped egg or eggs. Fry the roll again, in a non-stick frying pan preferably. Serve with chilli and tomato sauce.

Tip off
Spring Rolls can also be served with garlic soya dip.

Fried Chilli Chicken

Chilli Chicken is meant to be a hot dish not bland, so cook it, keeping this in mind.

Ingredients

800 gms chicken
2 tbsps flour
2 tsps arrowroot
1 or 2 eggs as per your choice
salt, oil, ajinomoto (spice)
ground white pepper and soya
sauce (to taste)

Fried Chilli Chicken

Method

Wash and clean the chicken with skin and cut it into eight to ten pieces. Whip the arrowroot, flour and egg together. Mix salt, ajinomoto and white pepper. Add two spoons of soya sauce. Cover the chicken pieces with this mixture and keep aside. Fry in oil. Take out the half-cooked pieces and fry again after a while. Place them on a plate. Garnish with soya sauce and fried onion rings before serving. Pieces of green chillies can also be used for garnishing as per your taste.

Tip off

Chilli Chicken can be served dry or with gravy depending upon your choice.

Chicken Sukiyaki

Japanese foods are freshly cooked without any chance for reheating hence they retain a natural flavour.

Chicken Sukiyaki

Ingredients

1 small cabbage
4 carrots
4-6 leaves of spinach
50 gms French beans
250 gms pork or chicken
some bean curd or tofu cheese
2 tsps soya sauce
¼ tsp ajinomoto
salt (to taste)
a pinch of ginger
250 gms rice noodles

Method

Cut the cabbage and carrots finely lengthwise. Cut the spinach and the French beans also. Partially boil the vegetables. Place a heater on the dining table and put a shallow container on it. Place the vegetables one by one separately, leaving the centre empty. Put the pieces of pork or chicken in the centre and soak it in the broth. Pieces of bean curd (a Japanese ingredient similar to cottage cheese or tofu cheese) should be uncooked but the rice noodles are to be dipped in boiling water and then taken out.

Sprinkle the soya sauce all over a thick bottomed vessel. Add ajinomoto, salt and a pinch of ginger as per taste. Arrange the vegetables, bean curd and rice noodles separately all along the container.

Tip off

Sukiyaki is cooked on the heater or oven, but nowadays, it is also cooked on gas stoves.

Vegetarian Sushi

Sushi is a Japanese food by tradition. While people may use the word, "sushi" when referring to raw fish, the term actually refers to seasoned cooked rice.

Vegetarian Sushi

Ingredients

½ cup rice vinegar
2 tbsps sesame oil
4 nori seaweed sheets
2 cups cooked short-grain rice
1 cup cucumber strips
1 cup cooked sweet potatoes
2 tbsp of toasted or fried
sesame seeds

Method

In a large mixing bowl, combine the rice vinegar with the sesame oil. Add the cucumber strips, stirring gently, and allow to marinate for about four hours. Remove from the marinade and drain. With a blender, whip the sweet potatoes until they are smooth and creamy. Lay a piece of plastic wrap on a flat surface. Place half a cup of rice on the plastic wrap and press to the size of a sheet of *nori*. Place a sheet of *nori* on top of rice, then spread ¼ or ½ cup of blended sweet potatoes on the *nori* and sprinkle with sesame seeds. Place ¼ or ½ cup cucumber strips in the middle. Roll up from the outside and dampen the edge to seal (the rice will be on the outside of the roll). Allow to chill for at least three hours before slicing. Slice with a damp knife into half-inch thick slices. Serve cold.

Tip off

For non-vegetarian, make the filling with meat or chicken, prawns, etc.

9 789350 578216